Science Matters
TELESCOPES

Jonathan Bocknek

WEIGL PUBLISHERS INC.

Published by Weigl Publishers Inc.
123 South Broad Street, Box 227
Mankato, MN USA 56002
Web site: www.weigl.com
Copyright ©2003 WEIGL PUBLISHERS INC.

Library of Congress Cataloging-in-Publication Data

Bocknek, Jonathan.
  Telescopes / Jonathan Bocknek.
     v. cm. -- (Science matters)
Includes index.
Contents: Getting to know telescopes -- Light, sight, and telescopes -- Types of telescopes -- What you can see with a telescope -- The Hubble space telescope -- Large telescopes on earth -- Telescopes in space -- Telescopes are time machines -- Surfing our solar system -- Science in action -- What have you learned?
  ISBN 1-59036-084-2 (lib. bdg. : alk. paper)
  1. Telescopes--Juvenile literature. [1. Telescopes.] I. Title. II. Series.
  QB88 .B63 2003
  522'.2--dc21

                    2002013851

Printed in the United States of America
1 2 3 4 5 6 7 8 9 0 06 05 04 03 02

       Project Coordinator Jennifer Nault **Substantive Editor** Heather Kissock
       Design Terry Paulhus **Copy Editor** Diana Marshall **Layout** Katherine Phillips
       Photo Researcher Peggy Chan

Photograph Credits

Contents

Studying Telescopes

How many stars are in the night sky? About 3,000 stars can be seen with the human eye from Earth. Still, **astronomers** know that there are millions of stars in space. How do they know this? Astronomers use telescopes to help them see stars and other space objects. Telescopes are instruments that **magnify** distant objects.

■ People have been viewing space objects through telescopes for hundreds of years.

Telescope Facts

Telescopes have helped astronomers in the discovery of some of the planets. Uranus, Neptune, and Pluto were all discovered using telescopes.

- The first known telescope was built in 1608. It was invented by Hans Lippershey, a Dutch eyeglass maker.

- An Italian astronomer is the first known person to turn a telescope toward the sky. His name was Galileo Galilei. He began using a telescope to study space in 1609.

- Galileo Galilei discovered four moons near Jupiter through a telescope.

- Galileo Galilei was the first person to see the rings of Saturn.

- Sir Isaac Newton invented the first **reflecting** telescope in 1668. This telescope used mirrors to collect light.

- Some of Earth's most powerful telescopes are located in Hawai'i.

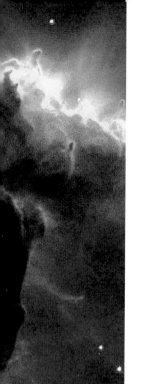

Light, Sight, and Telescopes

Telescopes make distant objects appear closer by collecting light. Telescopes can collect more light than the human eye can.

There are two main types of telescopes. A **refracting** telescope consists of two **lenses**. One lens collects the light of an object. The other lens magnifies the image so that it is clear.

A reflecting telescope collects the light of an object in the sky with a mirror. The light bounces off the mirror and onto a lens.

■ Telescopes with large mirrors collect more light than telescopes with small mirrors.

A Life of Science

Sir Isaac Newton

Sir Isaac Newton was born on December 25, 1642, in England. He is one of the most important scientists in history. Sir Isaac Newton built a new kind of telescope in 1668.

Sir Isaac Newton invented the first reflecting telescope. This telescope used mirrors in place of lenses. He observed the **satellites** of Jupiter through the telescope. Today, this invention is known as the Newtonian reflecting telescope.

Space Discoveries

Only six planets were known to exist in our solar system for a long period of time. People could view Mercury, Venus, Mars, Jupiter, and Saturn from Earth. Uranus was discovered in 1781 with the aid of a telescope. Telescopes were also used in the discoveries of Neptune and Pluto. Astronomers found Neptune in 1846. They discovered Pluto in 1930.

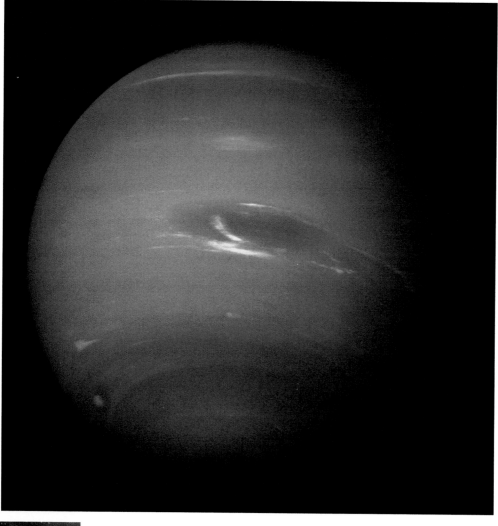

■ Neptune was discovered when scientists looked for another planet beyond Uranus.

A Life of Science
Caroline and William Herschel

Caroline and William Herschel lived in England during the 1700s. Caroline was William's sister. William was a music teacher, and Caroline was a mathematician. They both loved to observe space. They studied space through a telescope.

One night, Caroline and William noticed a dot of light in the sky. They had never seen this light before. They watched the movement of this dot for 6 months. It seemed to move like a planet. William and Caroline had discovered a new planet. Today, this planet is known as Uranus.

William Herschel

A Clearer View

Astronomers use large telescopes to observe space objects. Planets, stars, and entire **galaxies** can be observed through telescopes. Details of the Moon's surface are difficult to see from Earth. This is because the human eye cannot see that far into the distance. A telescope can show much more of the Moon's surface. Mountains, valleys, and **craters** are clearly seen when the Moon is viewed through a telescope.

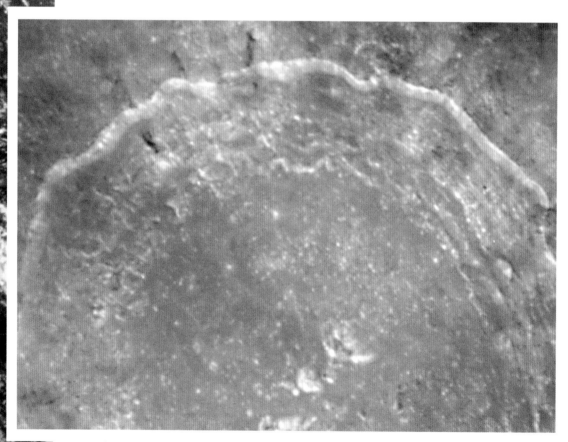

■ The *Hubble Space Telescope* took this photograph of one of the Moon's craters. This crater is called Copernicus.

Space Watchers

Astronomers are trained to study space. They spend many hours looking at the sky for answers to their questions. Still, astronomers are not the only people who are interested in space.

Amateur space watchers observe the night sky through telescopes. This sometimes leads to discoveries. Small objects circling the Sun between Mars and Jupiter were discovered this way. These objects were new asteroids. Space watchers also discovered another kind of space object. These objects seemed to have tails like tadpoles. They were undiscovered comets.

An important discovery was made by one space watcher. An Australian named Bob Evans discovered thirty-five new **supernovas**.

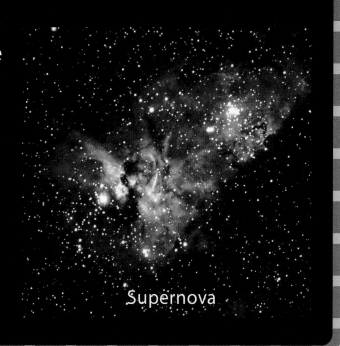

Supernova

Solar System Map

Match each planet on the left to its orbit in the diagram. This will show you the order of the planets in our solar system.

- Mercury
- Venus
- Earth
- Mars
- Jupiter
- Saturn
- Uranus
- Neptune
- Pluto

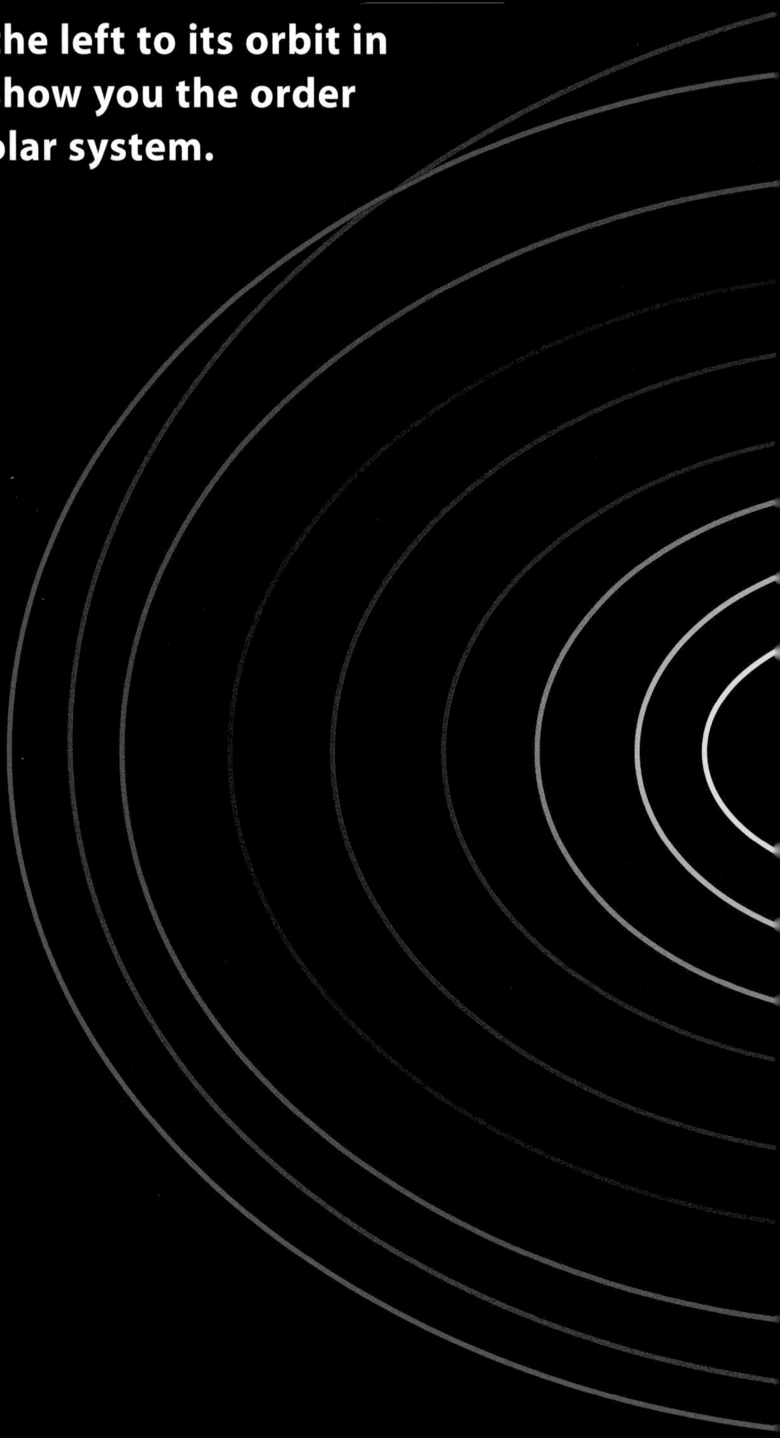

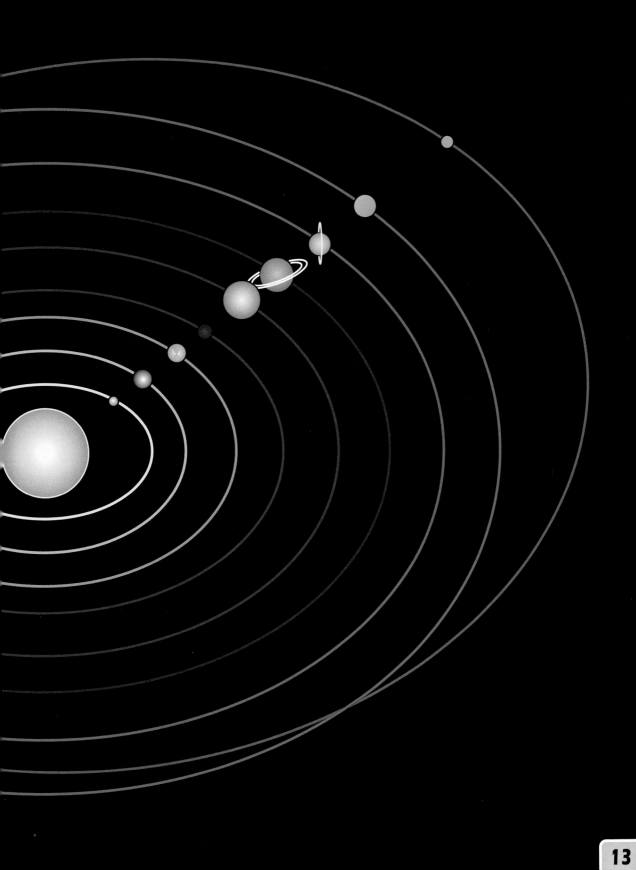

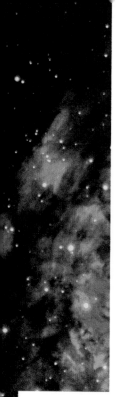

Telescopes on Earth

The aperture is an important part of a telescope. An aperture is the opening that allows light to enter the telescope. A large aperture can collect more light than a small aperture. This is why astronomers study space in observatories. These dome-shaped buildings contain telescopes that have large apertures. A special camera takes photographs of space objects as they appear through the telescope.

■ The Cerro Tololo Interamerican Observatory is located in Chile. Its large telescope is inside a silver dome.

The Largest Telescopes

Large telescopes are often located on or near the tops of mountains. This is because light in the sky is more clearly seen from high places. Also, it is easier to collect light away from cities and towns. This is why large telescopes are often built on mountains.

The Largest Telescopes on Earth

Telescope Name	Aperture Size	Location
VLT (Very Large Telescope)	52.5 feet (16 m)	Chile
Keck and Keck II	33 feet (10 m) each	Hawai'i
Hobby–Eberly	30 feet (9 m)	Texas
Subaru	27 feet (8 m)	Hawai'i
Gemini North and Gemini South	26 feet (8 m) each	Hawai'i and Chile
MMT (Multiple Mirror Telescope)	21 feet (6.5 m)	Arizona
Hale	16.5 feet (5 m)	California

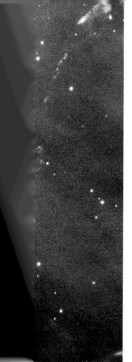

Telescopes in Space

Stars appear to twinkle in the night sky. This effect is caused by Earth's **atmosphere**. The Earth's atmosphere also affects large telescopes. There is only one place where a telescope is not affected by Earth's atmosphere. This place is above Earth's atmosphere. The *Hubble Space Telescope* is a spacecraft and a telescope. It allows astronomers to see space more clearly than ever before.

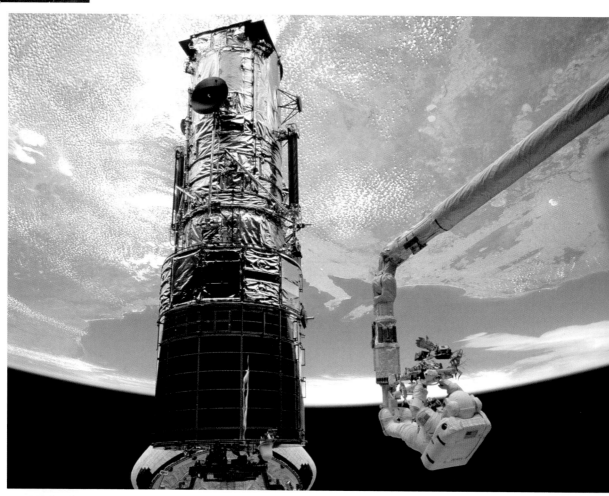

■ The *Hubble Space Telescope* is as large as a school bus. It travels about 375 miles (604 km) above Earth.

Hubble Highlights

The *Hubble Space Telescope* has photographed some incredible events in space. Most of these events would never have been seen without this invention. There have been many *Hubble* highlights.

- The *Hubble Space Telescope* took photographs of a comet colliding with Jupiter.

- The *Hubble Space Telescope* has taken the clearest photograph of Mars from Earth.

- Photographs taken by *Hubble* allowed astronomers to create the first map of Pluto's surface.

- The *Hubble Space Telescope* has taken images of the births and deaths of stars.

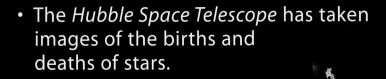

Time and Telescopes

Most of the objects in the sky are very far away. Light from these objects takes a long time to reach Earth. The closest star to Earth is the Sun. The second-closest star to Earth is called Proxima Centauri. Its light takes 4 years to reach Earth. When Proxima Centauri is viewed through a telescope, the image shows how it looked 4 years ago.

Most stars are much farther away from Earth than Proxima Centauri. Their light takes thousands of years to reach Earth.

■ Photographs of galaxies are often taken through telescopes. Billions of stars can be seen this way.

Light-Years Away

Objects are not always what they appear to be in space. The time it takes light to travel affects what we see in space.

A light-year is the distance light travels in 1 year. This distance is 6 trillion miles (9.7 trillion km). This is a very far distance. Most stars are even farther away.

The *Hubble Space Telescope* can view objects about 10 billion light-years away. This means that the *Hubble Space Telescope* can view 10 billion years into the past.

Surfing Our Solar System

How can I find more information about space?
- Libraries have many interesting books about space.
- Science centers are great places to learn about space.
- The Internet offers some great Web sites dedicated to space.

Where can I find a good reference Web site to learn more about space?
Encarta Homepage
www.encarta.com
- Type any space-related term into the search engine. Some terms to try include "light-year" and "galaxy."

How can I find out more about space, rockets, and astronauts?
NASA Kids
http://kids.msfc.nasa.gov
- This Web site offers puzzles and games, along with the latest news on NASA's research.

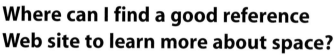

Science in Action

Make a Water Drop Lens

A magnifying glass is not the only thing that can make objects appear larger than they really are. Put one small drop of water onto a plastic or glass slide. Place the piece of plastic over a page of a newspaper. What do you see through the water drop? Hold the piece of plastic above the page. What do you see now? Add more water to the drop. How has the size of the letters on the page changed?

Compare the View

The telescope and the microscope were both invented around the year 1600. Research some books and the Internet to find out why scientists use microscopes. Divide a piece of paper into two columns. Compare microscopes and telescopes. Write down their similarities and their differences. Design a poster to share what you discover with your classmates.

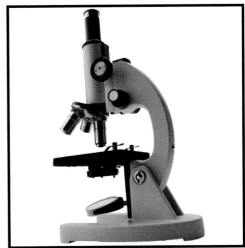

What Have You Learned?

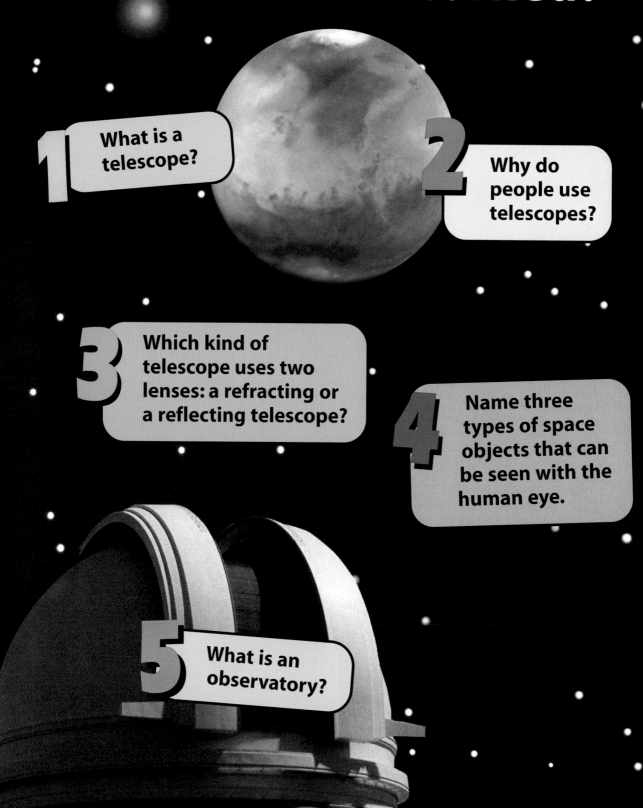

1 What is a telescope?

2 Why do people use telescopes?

3 Which kind of telescope uses two lenses: a refracting or a reflecting telescope?

4 Name three types of space objects that can be seen with the human eye.

5 What is an observatory?

6 Why are most observatories built near the tops of mountains?

7 Where would you find the *Hubble Space Telescope?*

8 How far is a light-year?

9 How many light-years from Earth is the star Proxima Centauri?

10 How have telescopes helped people learn more about space and the universe?

Answers: 1. An instrument that makes distant objects appear larger **2.** To see space objects that the human eye cannot see from Earth **3.** Refracting telescopes use two lenses. Reflecting telescopes use a mirror and a lens. **4.** Planets, stars, and galaxies **5.** A dome-shaped building containing a large telescope **6.** To see more light in the night sky **7.** Nearly 375 miles (604 km) above Earth's atmosphere **8.** 6 trillion miles (9.7 trillion km) **9.** 4 light years **10.** By allowing space objects to be seen from Earth

amateur: a person who does something for pleasure

astronomers: people who study space and its objects

atmosphere: the layer of gases surrounding a planet

craters: hollow areas on the surface of a planet

galaxies: large groups of stars

lenses: curved, clear pieces of glass or plastic that bend light rays to make objects appear larger than they are

magnify: make an object appear larger

reflecting: turning or throwing back an image

refracting: bending from a straight course to change direction

satellites: space objects that orbit another space object

supernovas: stars that explode when they get to the end of their lives

Index